FOR MY DAUGHTER

Small Book – Huge Thoughts

WOODWIND PRESS

Date

Date

Date

Date

Date

Date

Date

Date

Date

Date

Date

Date

Date

Date

Date

Date

Date

Date

Date

Date

Date

Date

Date

Date

Date

Date

Date

Date

Date

Date

Date

Date

Date

Date

Date

Date

Date

Date

Date

Date

Date

Date

Date

Date

Date

Date

Date

Date

Date

www.ingramcontent.com/pod-product-compliance
Lightning Source LLC
Chambersburg PA
CBHW021206020426
42331CB00003B/231